图书在版编目（CIP）数据

两栖动物 /（英）哥瑞斯·琼斯著；邢敏娟译 . —西安：世界图书出版西安有限公司，2018.1
（我的动物朋友）
ISBN 978-7-5192-3775-2

Ⅰ.①两… Ⅱ.①哥… ②邢… Ⅲ.①两栖动物—青少年读物 ②两栖动物—少年读物 Ⅳ.① Q959.5-49

中国版本图书馆 CIP 数据核字（2017）第 275792 号

First published in England in 2017 by Booklife Publishing.
Text and illustrations copyright © 2017 Booklife Publishing.
Bilingual: English-Simplified Chinese translation copyright © 2017 by World Publishing Xi'an Co. Ltd.
Bilingual: English-Simplified Chinese audio, video and APP copyright © 2017 by World Publishing Xi'an Co. Ltd.
All rights reserved.
本书仅限中国大陆地区发行销售。

书　　名	两栖动物（我的动物朋友）
著　　者	[英] 哥瑞斯·琼斯
译　　者	邢敏娟
策划编辑	陈宇彤
责任编辑	陈宇彤
装帧设计	新纪元文化传播
出版发行	世界图书出版西安有限公司
地　　址	西安市北大街 85 号
邮　　编	710003
电　　话	029-87214941　87233647（市场营销部）
	029-87234767（总编室）
网　　址	http://www.wpcxa.com
邮　　箱	xast@wpcxa.com
经　　销	新华书店
印　　刷	鹤山雅图仕印刷有限公司
开　　本	787mm×1092mm　1/12
印　　张	4
字　　数	20 千字
版　　次	2018 年 1 月第 1 版　2018 年 1 月第 1 次印刷
版权登记	25-2017-0060
国际书号	ISBN 978-7-5192-3775-2
定　　价	45.00 元

版权所有　翻印必究
（如有印装错误，请与出版社联系）

我的动物朋友

两栖动物

[英]哥瑞斯·琼斯/著
邢敏娟/译

动物王国

世界图书出版公司
西安 北京 上海 广州

本书英文原版为英国国家图书馆馆藏图书。本书与英国、美国、加拿大三大英语系国家同步出版。

目录

第 4–5 页

什么是生物?

第 6–7 页

什么是两栖动物?

第 8–9 页

它们的栖息地

第 10–11 页

两栖动物的家园

第 12–13 页

它们的食性

第 14–15 页

它们如何呼吸?

第 16–17 页

它们如何行动?

第 18–19 页

它们如何生长?

第 20–21 页

令人惊叹的两栖动物

第 22–23 页

打破世界纪录的两栖动物

什么是生物？

所有的生物都具有生长、发育、繁殖的能力。
生物需要空气、营养、水和阳光。

这些都是生物。

青蛙　　老虎　　人类

刀，叉，
盘子。

书

这些都是
非生物。

非生物不具有生长、发育、繁殖的能力。非生物不需要空气、营养、水或阳光，因为它们没有生命气息。

泰迪熊

5

什么是两栖动物？

两栖动物是可以在水中和陆地上生存的生物。它们的生存离不开空气、食物、水和阳光。青蛙、蝾螈和蟾蜍，都属于两栖动物。

青蛙

蟾蜍

蝾螈

大多数两栖动物拥有四肢和蹼足。它们是冷血动物，它们的体温会随着外界温度的变化而变化。

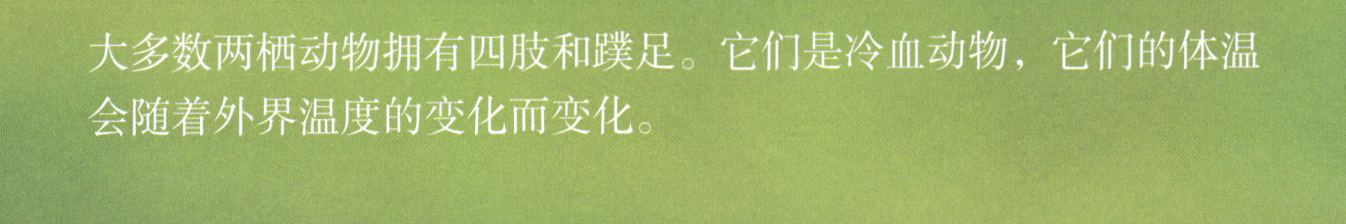

腿

蹼足

资料：

我们已知的两栖动物有 7000 多种。

7

它们的栖息地

所有的生物都有它们的**栖息地**或家园。两栖动物生活在水边或者潮湿的地方，包括小溪、森林、草地、沼泽、湿地、池塘、雨林和湖泊。

森林

大多数两栖动物的幼体生活在水中，因为它们此时还没有肺，无法在陆地上呼吸。

青蛙的幼体，称为蝌蚪。

两栖动物的家园

两栖动物生活在世界上不同的栖息地。青蛙和蟾蜍常常生活在淡水池塘中。芦苇给它们以庇护，帮助它们远离**捕食者**的威胁。池塘里的昆虫则是它们很好的食物。

一些两栖动物生活在气候炎热的地方，例如雨林。雨林中每年雨水丰沛，这给两栖动物提供了湿润的气候环境。

它们的食性

几乎所有的成年两栖动物都是**食肉动物**。它们大都吃昆虫、蠕虫、蛞蝓甚至是老鼠一类的小动物。它们利用它们超级灵敏的嗅觉在夜间外出捕食。

巴西树蛙是已知的唯一一种以水果和浆果为食的蛙类。

两栖动物用它们长而黏的舌头来捕食。它们用强壮的后腿来迅速跳跃,从而出其不意捕获猎物。

强壮的后腿

黏黏的舌头

资料:
两栖动物不需要**喝水**,因为它们可以通过皮肤摄取水分。

一只红眼树蛙伸出舌头捕捉蝴蝶

它们如何呼吸？

大部分两栖动物都是通过肺和皮肤呼吸。它们通过皮肤获取氧气然后输送至全身。

资料：
它们的皮肤必须保持湿润，以便能够获取氧气。

蝌蚪

腮

一些两栖动物，比如蝌蚪，在身体两侧都长有腮，在水中它们用腮进行呼吸。随着它们逐渐长大，它们会长出肺，这使得它们也能够在陆地上呼吸。

它们如何 行动？

火蝾螈

长长的身躯

尾巴

短小的四肢

像蝾螈这样长有尾巴的两栖动物，一般都拥有长长的身躯和短小无力的四肢。这意味着它们不能跑得很快，只能像蛇一样向前移动。

像青蛙和蟾蜍这样的无尾两栖动物，都有着短而宽的身体和强壮的后腿。它们的后腿通常比前腿大三倍，这使得它们能够跳得很高。

没有尾巴

短小的身体

强壮的后腿

一只正在跳跃的角蛙

它们如何生长？

蛙卵

青蛙的卵叫蛙卵

大部分两栖动物都是卵生动物,这些卵经孵化成为生活在水中的蝌蚪或幼虫。在这个阶段,它们会进食大量植物性食物,以便能够快速生长。

两栖动物幼体时期肺部开始生长发育，这使得它们能够在陆地上呼吸。这时它们不再进食植物性食物，取而代之的是昆虫。它们继续生长发育直至完全成年，这个过程需要花费几周甚至是一年多的时间。

一只刚刚孵化出来的小蝾螈

一只成年蓝色斑点蝾螈

令人惊叹的两栖动物

两栖动物色彩艳丽。红眼树蛙居住在南美的雨林中，它们有着红色的眼睛、橙色的脚趾和蓝绿色的身体。

资料：

成群结队的青蛙被称为"蛙群"。

蛙类色彩艳丽的皮肤向其他动物发出了警告：食用有毒、危险。这使得它们免于被捕食者捕食。

一些雌性蝾螈会把卵产在陆地上并且会一直保护着它们，直到孵化成功。同时，为了照顾这些卵，妈妈们通常会不吃不睡。

打破世界纪录的两栖动物

中国大鲵 俗名娃娃鱼

纪录： 中国大鲵是世界上*最大*的两栖动物。

资料： 中国大鲵生活在湖泊中。中国大鲵是中国特有的珍稀野生动物。

尺寸： 身体长达 1.8米

玻璃蛙

纪录:
世界上最不可思议的两栖动物。

资料:
玻璃蛙的身体几乎是透明的。你能看到青蛙的内部吗？

尺寸:
身长2厘米

2cm
实际身长!

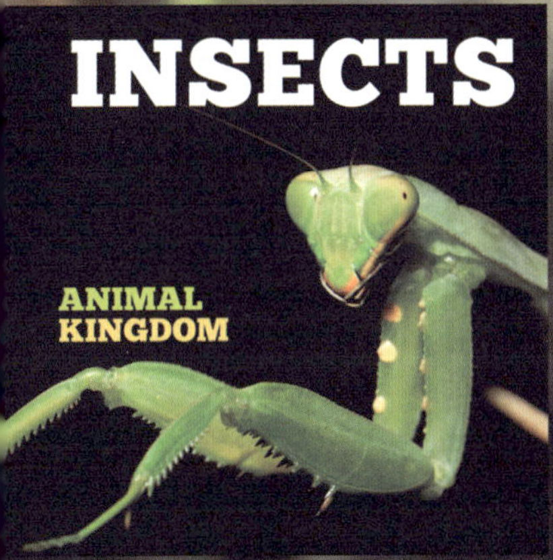

ANIMAL KINGDOM

What is a living thing? Where do animals live? What do animals eat? How do they move and grow? Learn the answers to these questions in this exciting new series. With easy to read text and informative diagrams, this series offers a simple introduction to the animals that live in our world.

REPTILES
ANIMAL KINGDOM

FISH
ANIMAL KINGDOM

INSECTS
ANIMAL KINGDOM

MAMMALS
ANIMAL KINGDOM

BIRDS
ANIMAL KINGDOM

AMPHIBIANS
ANIMAL KINGDOM

Glossary

Carnivores: animals that eat other animals rather than plants.

Climates: types of weather in particular places.

Habitat: a home where animals and plants live.

Hatch: when a baby animal or insect comes out of its egg.

Larvae: an insect or animal's young.

Predators: any animal that eats other animals and insects.

Prey: any animal or insect that is eaten by another.

Index

Breathe 9, 14, 15, 19
Food 6, 10, 13, 18
Frogs 6, 10, 12, 13, 17, 18, 20, 23
Grow 4, 5, 15, 18, 19
Homes 8, 10
Living Things 4, 6, 8
Move 14, 16
Salamanders 6, 16, 19, 21, 22
Toads 6, 10, 17
Water 4, 5, 6, 8, 9, 13, 15, 18

Photo Credits

Photocredits: Abbreviations: l–left, r–right, b–bottom, t–top, c–centre, m–middle. All images are courtesy of Shutterstock.com.

Front Cover - Irina Kozorog, 1 - kazoka, 2-3 - Dynamicfoto, 4bl - Chros, 4c - Eric Isselee, 4r - michaeljung, 5bl - Elena Schweitzer, 5tl - koosen, 5r - Lichtmeister, 6bl - Vitalii Hulai, 6br - Hintau Aliaksei, 6tr - Tsekhmister, 7 - Tremor Photography, 8 - Quick Shot, 9 - Napat, 10 - Svetlana Foote, 1 - Fotos593, 12 - Ricardo de Paula Ferreira, 13, 15bc - Cathy Keifer, 14 - Ioloi, 15tl - Philipyb Studio, 16 - Valerio Pardi, 17– muhamad mizan bin ngateni, 18 - Ian Grainger, 19 - Sheila Fitzgerald, 19br - Michiel de Wit, 20 - Dirk Ercken, 21 - Choke29, 22 - WikiCommons_KYOTO_AQUARIUM13, 23 - Dr. Morley Read, 24 - IsiGallery, 25 - schimmery

24

GLASS FROG

Record: The World's Weirdest Amphibian

Fact: The Glass Frog is completely see through. What can you see inside the frog?

Size: 2cm long

2cm — Actual size!

World Record Breakers

CHINESE GIANT SALAMANDER

Record: The World's Biggest Amphibian

Fact: Chinese giant salamanders live in lakes. It is a rare wild animal in China.

Size: Up to 1.8 metres long

22

Some female salamanders lay their eggs on land and protect them until they hatch. While they are looking after their eggs, the mothers do not eat or sleep.

Amazing Amphibians

Amphibians can be very colourful. The Red-Eyed Tree frog lives in the rainforests of South America and has red eyes, orange toes and a green and blue body.

Fact:
A group of frogs is called an "army".

The frogs' brightly coloured skin warns other animals that it is poisonous or dangerous if eaten. This stops them being eaten by predators.

The young amphibians begin to grow lungs so they can breathe on land and eat insects instead of plants. They continue to grow and change until they are fully-grown adults. This can take anywhere from a few weeks to more than a year.

A newly hatched salamander.

An adult Blue-Spotted Salamander.

How Do They Grow?

Frogspawn

Frogs' eggs are called frogspawn.

Most amphibians start life as eggs that **hatch** into tadpoles or **larvae** that live in water. At this stage, they eat lots of plant food so they can grow big and strong.

Tailless amphibians, like frogs and toads, have short, wider bodies and strong back legs. Their back legs are usually three times larger than their front legs, which means they can jump very high.

No Tail

Short Body

Strong Back Legs

Jumping Pacman Frog

How Do They **Move**?

Long Body

Fire Salamander

Tail

Short Legs

Amphibians with tails, like salamanders, usually have long bodies and short, weak legs. This means that they can't run very quickly but move in a similar way to a snake.

Tadpoles

Gills

Some amphibians, like tadpoles, have gills on either side of their bodies which they use to breathe with under the water. When they are older, they grow lungs which enables them breathe on land too.

How Do They Breathe?

Most amphibians breathe through their lungs and their skin. Oxygen is absorbed through the skin and then moves around the rest of the body.

Fact:
Their skin must be wet for them to be able to absorb oxygen.

Amphibians have long, sticky tongues which they use to catch their food. They also have strong back legs so they can jump quickly and take their prey by surprise.

Strong Back Legs

Sticky Tongue

Fact: Amphibians don't need to drink any water because they take it in through their skin.

A Red-Eyed Tree frog sticks out his tongue to catch a butterfly.

What Do They Eat?

Nearly all adult amphibians are carnivores. They mostly eat insects, worms, slugs and even small animals, like mice. They use their super sense of smell to hunt out prey at night-time.

The Brazilian Tree frog is the only known frog to eat fruits and berries.

Some amphibians live in hotter climates, such as rainforests. Rainforests get a lot of rain every year, providing a wet climate for amphibians to live in.

Amphibian Homes

Amphibians live in many different habitats around the world. A common habitat for frogs and toads are freshwater ponds. The reeds provide them with shelter from **predators** and the insects in the pond provide them with food to eat.

Most amphibians live in the water when they are very young. This is because they do not yet have lungs to be able to breathe air on land.

Young frogs, called tadpoles.

Where Do They Live?

All living things live in a **habitat** or home. Amphibians live near to water or in damp places, including streams, forests, meadows, bogs, swamps, ponds, rainforests and lakes.

Forest

Most amphibians have four legs and webbed feet. They are cold-blooded animals. This means that their body temperature changes when the temperature outside is hotter or colder.

Legs

Webbed Feet

Fact: There are over 7,000 known species of amphibian.

What Is an Amphibian?

Amphibians are living things that can live in the water and on land. They need air, food, water and sunlight to live. Frogs, salamanders and toads are all types of amphibians.

Frog

Toad

Salamander

Knife, fork & plate.

Books

These are all non-living things.

Non-living things do not have the ability to grow, develop and reproduce. Non-living things do not need air, nutrition, water or sunlight because they are not alive.

Teddy Bear

What Are Living Things?

All living things have the ability to grow, develop and reproduce. Living things need air, nutrition, water and sunlight to stay alive.

These are all living things.

Frog

Tiger

Human

4

contents

Pages 4-5
What Are Living Things?

Pages 6-7
What is an Amphibian?

Pages 8-9
Where Do They Live?

Pages 10-11
Amphibian Homes

Pages 12-13
What Do They Eat?

Pages 14-15
How Do They Breathe?

Pages 16-17
How Do They Move?

Pages 18-19
How Do They Grow?

Pages 20-21
Amazing Amphibians

Pages 22-23
World Record Breakers

Page 24
Glossary & Index

A catalogue record for this book is available from the British Library.

Words that appear like **this** can be found in the glossary on page 24.

AMPHIBIANS

Grace Jones

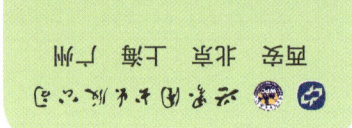

ANIMAL
KINGDOM

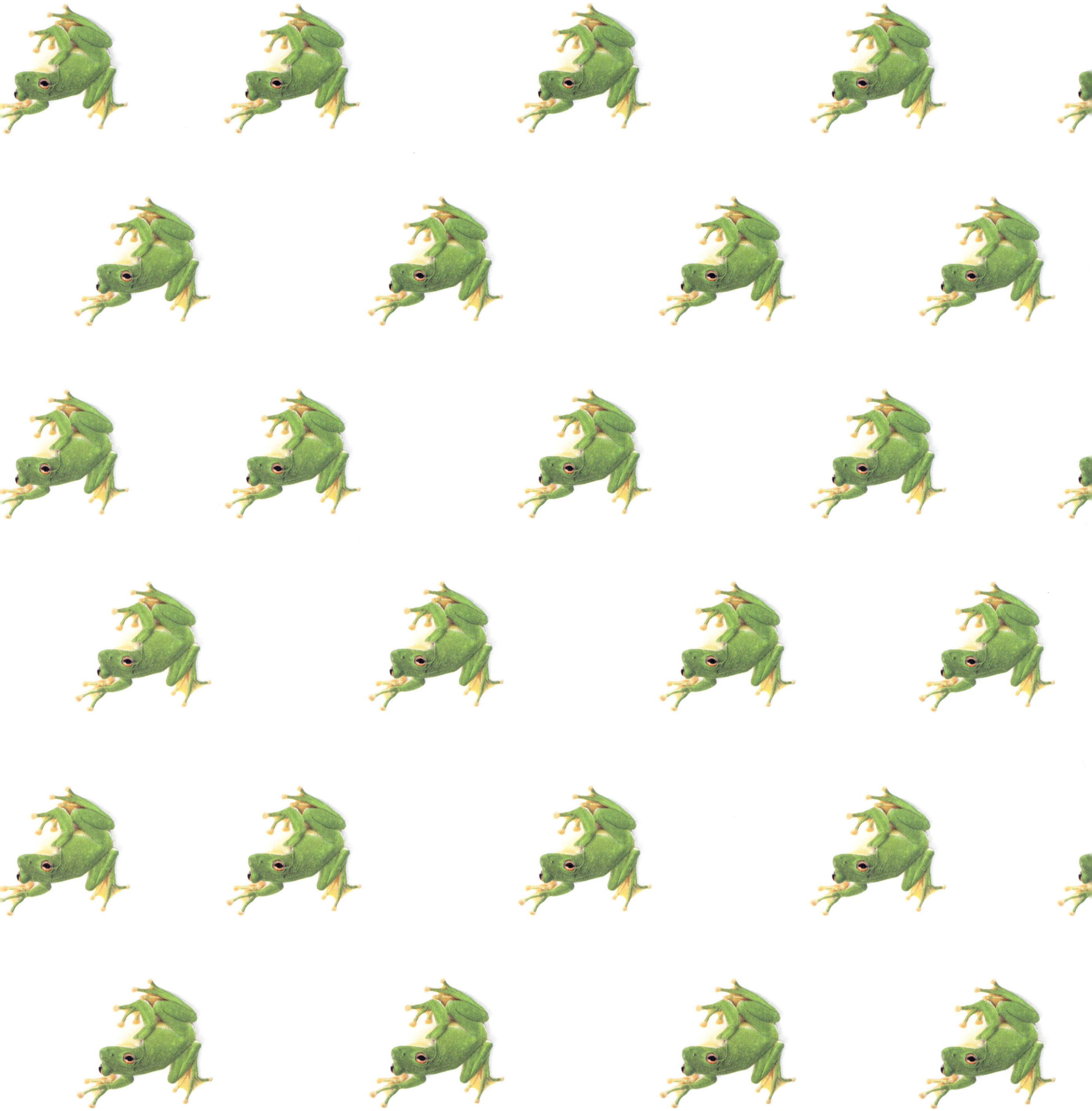